Kangaroo Mouse

KIDS EXPLORE!

Kangaroo Mouse

There are only two species of the Kangaroo Mouse. Kangaroo mice are also known as, 'gnome mice'. It is in the rodent family and gets its name from the way it moves about - something like a kangaroo. This little animal is very cute, yet very odd, which you will discover in greater detail. We are going to explore where this creature lives, its extraordinary abilities and so much more. Read on to be totally amazed with this cool creature.

Where in the World?

Did you know the Kangaroo Mouse is mostly found in Nevada? It is also found in the deserts of California, Nevada, Oregon, Utah and Idaho. These rodents like sandy desert areas. It will live among the scrub brush, where it forages for food and builds its long burrow.

The Body of a Kangaroo

Did you know the Kangaroo mouse has long back legs and short front legs? It has a large head, short neck and long whiskers. It also has a thick tail it uses for balance. Adult kangaroo mice only weigh about a half-ounce. They have large black eyes and big ears, as well.

The Fur of a Kangaroo

Did you know this rodent has silky fur? It also has fur-lined cheek pouches, which we will read more about later. The kangaroo mouse also has stiff hairs that fringe its hind feet. The bottom of its white feet are covered in thick fur, as well. This keeps its feet safe from the hot desert sand.

The Kangaroo Mouse Pouch

Did you know this rodent has cheek pouches like a hamster? The pouches of this rodent come in very handy when it is out foraging for food. Like a shopping bag, the kangaroo mouse can shove food inside these pouches to carry back to its burrow.

The Feet of a Kangaroo Mouse

Did you know this rodent has very long feet? The kangaroo mouse gets its name from the way it jumps - just like a kangaroo. This little mouse uses it powerful back legs and big feet to leap around. It is said that these little critters can jump around 2 to 3 feet (0.6 to 0.9 meters) in one leap.

The Burrows of the Kangaroo Mouse

Did you know this rodent can have large burrows? Its burrow can measure from 3 to 8 feet (1 to 2.5 meters). Some species like to burrow in fine sand, while others prefer gravel. During the daytime, this mouse covers the entrance to its burrow. This helps keep it safe from predators.

Kangaroo Mouse Behavior

Did you the kangaroo mouse is nocturnal? This means its sleeps all day. During the night time, this rodent will forage to food. It is much safer to be out at night, than during the day when you are this small. This animal also sleeps all winter long.

What a Kangaroo Mouse Eats

Did you know the kangaroo mouse eats a variety of foods? It will eat seeds and scrubby vegetation. This rodent also likes to eat meat. It will hunt and eat insects, as well as carrion. This means the animal is already dead. The kangaroo mouse will also store food away food in its burrow to eat later.

The Kangaroo Mouse's Special Ability

Did you know the kangaroo mouse does not need to drink water? To beat the desert heat, this mouse is mostly active at night. This keeps it from having to drink a lot of water. This rodent does not make a lot of urine, so it can conserve water. The kangaroo mouse also gets water from its food and the plant matter it dines on.

Kangaroo Mouse Mom

Did you know the mom kangaroo mouse has her babies in May to June? She gives birth to her young at the end of her underground burrow. The female builds a soft nest here, with stuff she has collected. Once the babies are born, she feeds them milk from her body.

The Baby Kangaroo Mouse

Did you know there can be anywhere from 2 to 7 kangaroo babies born at one time? These little creatures are born very small. However, they do have big feet and a long tail. Baby kangaroo mice are helpless as newborns. They are blind and also deaf. They depend on their mom for all their needs.

Predators of the Kangaroo Mouse

Did you know this animal has many natural predators? Animals like snakes, foxes, owls and badgers all hunt this tiny rodent. People are also harming the kangaroo mouse populations. This is because humans are taking over the kangaroo mouse's habitat. Some plants are also dangerous to this species of rodent.

Life of a Kangaroo Mouse

Did you know the kangaroo mouse has a short lifespan? Because they are so small, this animal does not have a long life. It will only live for about 2 to 3 years-of-age. This little fella likes to spend its time eating and sleeping and mostly likes to be left alone.

Pale Kangaroo Mouse

Did you know this kangaroo mouse is very light in color? That is where it got its name from. This little mouse is rarely seen. It has long, soft pale-colored fur. It measures around 6.2 inches long (16 centimeters). That does not include its really long tail.

Dark Kangaroo Mouse

Did you know this species of kangaroo mouse is darker in color? it has large black eyes, big ears and feet, with a long tail. It prefers to stay underground most of the day. In its burrow, the dark kangaroo mouse is thought to sleep on its back inside a well constructed nest.

Quiz

Question 1: How many species of the kangaroo mouse are there?

Answer 1: Only two

Question 2: Where can kangaroo mice be found?

Answer 2: In the desert regions, mostly in Nevada.

Question 3: How far can a kangaroo mouse leap?

Answer 3: 2 to 3 feet (0.6 to 0.9 meters)

Question 4: What is the kangaroo mouse's special ability?

Answer 4: It does not need to drink water

Question 5: Which kangaroo mouse is light in color?

Answer 5: The Pale Kangaroo Mouse

Thank you for checking out another title from Kids Explore! Make sure to check out Amazon.com for many other great books.

CPSIA information can be obtained at www.ICGtesting.com
Printed in the USA
LVIW01n1027100716
495759LV00023B/88